Around Kirkcaldy

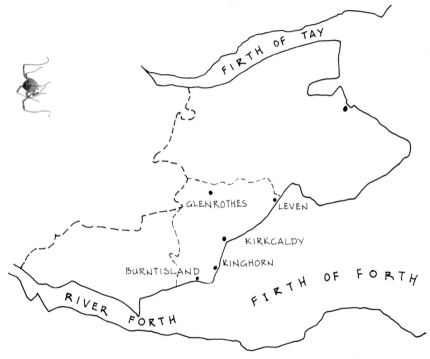

FIRTH OF TAY

GLENROTHES

LEVEN

KIRKCALDY

KINGHORN

BURNTISLAND

FIRTH OF FORTH

RIVER FORTH

The Kingdom of Fife

FIRST EDITION
Printed March 1993

" I'll tae Fife." - Macduff.

John MacMillan Pearson
© Copyright 1993
All rights reserved
ISBN· 0·9519134·3·3

Printed by :-
Levenmouth Printers,
Banbeath Place,
Leven, Fife.

Around Kirkcaldy

FIFE REGIONAL COUNCIL COAT OF ARMS

VIRTUTE ET OPERA

by John M. Pearson

Leslie House

This book takes a look at an area of Fife known as Kirkcaldy District as established in 1975 when local government reorganisation took place throughout Scotland. It is roughly a triangular area stretching along the shores of the Firth of Forth from Burntisland to Leven and then inland to the new town of Glenrothes. Kirkcaldy District is mainly an industrial area that benefited from the rich coal seams of Fife, a plentiful water supply and good harbour facilities for trade with Europe.

The heyday of the old industries such as salt, weaving, mining, fishing, shipbuilding, steel, linoleum and rail transport is long past and many industries have now disappeared altogether. This has affected the heart and soul of many communities which only existed because of a specific industry. Consequently many of the towns and villages fell into disrepair as industries closed down and people sought work elsewhere. To counter this a combination of massive redevelopment and a policy of investment has attracted new industrial growth. One of the most important initiatives was in establishing the new town of Glenrothes in 1948 along with industrial estates throughout Kirkcaldy District. This has encouraged new technology companies to set up here which revives prospects of a rosy future.

Kirkcaldy District is also rich in history and folklore and offers many recreational facilities for both the visitor and local resident.

THE NEW CALEDONIAN Hotel

THE NEW CALEDONIAN HOTEL

AA THREE STAR HOTEL —
PRIVATELY OWNED BY MR & MRS T. HERD

81, HIGH STREET, LEVEN. KY8 4NG
tel. 0333 424101   fax. 0333 421241

Burntisland Library

6

Burntisland lies sandwiched between the Binn, a 200m. high hill, and the Firth of Forth and its close association with the sea has been crucial to its prosperity and survival down through the centuries. The strategic importance of this area has been recognised since the days of Roman invasion, and the advantages of good harbour facilities surely influenced the Roman Commander, Agricola when he reputedly set up camp on nearby Dunearn Hill.

In the early 12th century Burntisland Castle was built and the church at Kirkton was founded at the foot of the Binn. The first permanent settlement in the area formed around the church and was known as Wester Kingorne, which was controlled by the Abbots of Dunfermline until the 16th century. It was then in 1541 that King James V granted Burntisland its charter as a Royal Burgh, with the main intention of developing the harbour facilities into a naval port. Royalty often visited the town while passing en route from Edinburgh to their favourite retreat at Falkland Palace. Of special note was the visit of King Charles I in 1633 who had travelled north from London to be crowned in Scotland. After the coronation Charles embarked on a tour of his Royal Palaces and the entourage visited Burntisland on the return journey to Edinburgh. On crossing over to Leith the boat with the Royal Household goods and treasure sunk in a sudden, violent storm. The treasure has never been recovered although many have tried. Other famous names associated with Burntisland are Vice Admiral Fairfax, Mary Somerville and Thomas Chalmers.

An increasing population in the late 16th century created a demand for a new Parish Church which was built overlooking the harbour in 1592. It still stands today and is the oldest Post Reformation Church in Scotland still in use. In 1601 King James VI ordered the General Assembly to meet in this Church and it was then proposed that there be a new translation of the Bible. This was known as the Authorised Version which was published in 1611. Between 1651 and 1660 Cromwell's forces occupied Burntisland and the iron grip of the invading forces strangled the town's trade and prosperity. In spite of this, Burntisland recovered and even though similar slumps in fortune have occurred, the town has always bounced back to make the most of any profitable opportunity. Between the 17th and 20th century various events such as the increased herring catches, the coming of the railway, the coal industry, ship-building and the establishment of British Alcan Aluminium Ltd. have all contributed to lifting the town out of lean economic times.

Today Burntisland is one of Fife's three main ports, alongside Kirkcaldy and Methil, which plays a key role in the local economy. There is also a dock area which has a large fabrication shed for the construction of components for the offshore oil and gas industry and British Alcan is still a major force. Of equal importance to Burntisland are the famous Links and sandy beaches and the highlights of the year are the annual Highland Games in July and the summer fair and shows.

Parish Church

7

Cuinzie Neuk - possible site of old Royal Mint

Kinghorn was a favourite resort with Royalty and from 1200 onwards formed part of the dowry granted by the Scots' Kings to their Queens. In 1286 a royal tragedy outside Kinghorn left the Scots throne with no real successor. On a stormy March night Alexander III set out from Edinburgh to visit his Queen Yolande at Kinghorn Tower. The Ferrymen at Queensferry reluctantly set sail for Fife at the Royal command, and disregarding further warnings the Royal party continued on towards Kinghorn. As they were clambering up a narrow path leading up to the cliffs between Burntisland and Kinghorn Alexander became separated from the rest of the party. In the pitch dark the horse stumbled sending Alexander plunging to his death. It was a national calamity as his successor, the young Maid of Norway, died soon after. With no recognised contender to the Scots throne, Edward I of England, the 'Hammer of the Scots', battled for many years to gain control of Scotland. Ultimately Scotland won its fight for independence at the decisive Battle of Bannockburn in 1314. A monument to Alexander III was erected in 1887 near to the spot where he fell to his death in 1286. Kinghorn remained a Royal residence until the reign of Robert II when it was granted to Sir John Lyon as a dowry on his marriage to Janet Stuart - the King's daughter. Many years later in 1767 John Lyon, the 8th Earl of Strathmore and Kinghorn married Mary Bowes, daughter of Sir George Bowes. He had left his daughter a fortune and one condition of his will was that she had to incorporate her name with the name of her husband, hence the name Bowes-Lyon.

Initially Kinghorn had developed around both the harbour and Loch Burn which flows from the Kinghorn Loch. When Royalty left Kinghorn, the town declined in importance and it was not until the early 19th century that Kinghorn's fortunes revived. James Ayton tried unsuccessfully to set up a flax mill in 1792 but shortly afterwards other local entrepreneurs, including William Swan, had established a thriving business. The new flax mills were of great benefit to the community up to their closure in the 1880's. A candlemaking factory opened up in 1886 in one of the old mills but had closed by 1893. Then nearly thirty years later a leather works took over the premises. It was an era of great initiative and production. In 1902 William Gibson set up a 'Cleek Works' - a golf club factory at the Bow Butts. It was a great success and by 1913 he had moved to larger premises in Baliol St. Eventually the firm hit hard times and closed in 1955. The Kinghorn Golf Club was formed in 1887 and it was not until 1894 that the Golf Course was built. The first 9 hole course was designed by the famous Tom Morris and in 1905 the course was extended to 18 holes.

"There's mony speir the road to Kinghorn and ken it a' the way to Pettycur Ferry." This local saying highlights the fact that while both Kinghorn and Pettycur were adjacent it was Pettycur that was the more important as the ferry port to Newhaven. The main stagecoach routes from the north of Fife were timed to connect with the ferry crossings.

Corner of Eastgate and North Overgate

9

In 1846-47 the Burntisland - Kinghorn section of the railway was constructed with a spur line to Pettycur harbour. With good road, rail and ferry facilities this was a huge benefit to industries sprouting up in the Kinghorn area. For instance a saltworks was built near Pettycur harbour in 1870. This closed in 1894 but a small bottleworks was then built on this site in 1902. Even though the bottleworks closed down that same year it reopened in 1908 to make bottles for whisky companies until 1982. Kinghorn became heavily involved in shipbuilding and while the yards closed in 1909 they opened again between 1919 and 1922 to build passenger ships. The last ship to be built at the yards was the S.S. Kinghorn in 1921.

The original Parish Church was consecrated in 1243 but the present Church dates from 1774. The famous soldier, Sir William Kirkcaldy of Grange (1520 -1573) lies buried in the Churchyard although the location of his grave is unknown. Sir William had a most chequered military career and in 1546 was involved in the assassination of Cardinal Beaton at St. Andrews. He was taken prisoner, and although sent over to France he managed to escape back to Scotland. On his return he fought with the Protestant army against Mary Queen of Scots. Later he changed sides and held Edinburgh Castle under siege for three years for his Queen. On surrendering the Castle he received no mercy from his enemies and was promptly executed.

10 Kinghorn Harbour

Kinghorn Coat of Arms

The highest point in the cemetery is known as the Witches' Hill. Over at the top of the cliffs is an iron ring fastened into a rock. This was where the witches were chained when they were being punished for their witchcraft. The last witch was burned at the stake here on 24th March, 1644. A high standing cross marks the grave of Mrs Burnett-Smith who wrote romantic stories and novels under the pseudonym of Annie S. Swan.

The Bow Butts was the area where the townsfolk practised their archery in medieval times. Today in the gardens of Bow Butts House stands a mid 18th century octagonal doocot which unusually has a basement that was used as an ice box.

Doocot - Bow Butts House, Kinghorn.

11

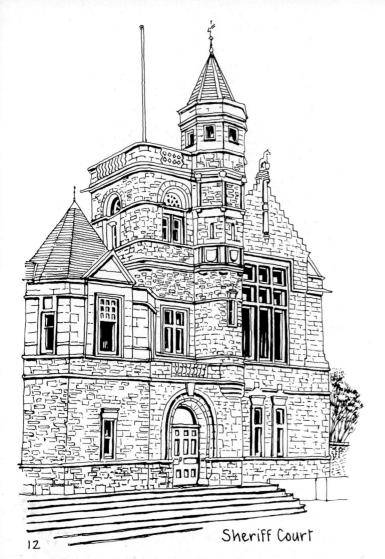

Sheriff Court

Kirkcaldy was one of Scotland's most ancient burghs and the meaning for its name has been lost in the distant past. As far back as 1075 Kirkcaldy was referred to as Kirkaladunt and later on as Kircalethin or Kirkaldin suggesting a possible link with the old Pictish language - Caer caled din - fort on the hard hill. The shire of Kirkaladunt was owned by the Crown until 1075, then the Church at Dunfermline until 1451 when control was handed over to the townsfolk. Over the years Kirkcaldy had developed a system of government whereby a select group of burgesses looked after the affairs of the Town. In 1469 an Act was passed by the Scots Parliament to abolish this closed shop. The burgesses, or Neighbours as they were named, perceived this as a threat to all their privileges. They adopted a thrawn attitude towards Parliament and in 1588 even passed a Resolution against the election of Provosts, which was required by law. In 1644 Kirkcaldy was created a Royal Burgh by Charles I but it was not until 1658, that Robert Whyte was elected the first Provost.

Throughout his reign Charles I tried to establish an absolute monarchy and episcopal Church. This led to virtual civil war and Kirkcaldy came out in support of the Covenanters, the King's enemies. At the Battle of Kilsyth in 1645 Kirkcaldy was well represented in the 6,000 strong army which was heavily defeated by Montrose. Further tragedy followed in 1651 when Cromwell's troops occupied Kirkcaldy and plundered the town's treasure.

The 19th century saw a great upsurge in industrial activity and Kirkcaldy became established as a major industrial centre. As the town expanded it swallowed up the neighbouring small villages from Linktown in the west, up to Pathhead and through Sinclairtown to the Gallatown. Not surprisingly Kirkcaldy became known as the Lang Toun.

In 1821 Kirkcaldy was the first town to use the powerloom which revolutionised the weaving industry. Kirkcaldy owed its prosperity to the initiative of certain key people. One of these was Michael Nairn. He was initially involved in the weaving of ships sails but diversified to manufacture floorcloths. At first he was ridiculed and his factory, which was built at Pathhead in 1847, was known as Nairn's Folly. Much to the surprise of his critics his venture proved a great success. Before long other factories were built, and by 1876 they were manufacturing linoleum which was to make Kirkcaldy famous worldwide. The use of linseed oil in the production of linoleum resulted in a distinctive smell which hung over the town. This was highlighted in a well known poem 'The Boy in the train' which was written by Mary Campbell Smith in 1913.

"I'll sune be ringin' ma Gran'ma's bell,
She'll cry, "Come ben, my laddie."
For I ken mysel' by the queer-like smell
That the next stop's Kirkcaddy!"

M.C.S.

Sailors' Walk, Kirkcaldy.

Pathhead House

The rich owners of the linoleum business generously ploughed back their profits into improving the amenities of Kirkcaldy. The Nairn Family donated funds to build a school, a hospital, the Museum Art Gallery and Public Library. They also donated Ravenscraig Park; Michael Beveridge, another successful linoleum manufacturer donated the vast grounds of Beveridge Park and Robert Philp, a linen manufacturer left £70,000 for educational purpose.

Other famous people born in Kirkcaldy include Adam Smith the economist, Robert Adam the architect, George Gillespie - Moderator of the General Assembly, John Ritchie who took control of the Scotsman newspaper, Marjorie Fleming the child poet, Sir Sandford Fleming the great railway engineer and Michael Scott, the Wizard of the North in the 13th century from Balweari.

Adam Smith (1723-90) wrote his famous book 'Inquiry Into the Nature and Causes of the Wealth of Nations' which was published in 1776. The book set out a new approach to economics and the theories are often expounded on by modern economists. Smith lived at 220, High Street and although the house has been demolished, a close nearby has been named after him. In 1899 Andrew Carnegie opened the Adam Smith Hall. It was modernised in 1973 and renamed the Adam Smith Centre. The inaugural event to open the Centre was the Adam Smith Commemorative Symposium which marked the 250th anniversary of his birth.

Robert Adam was born at Gladney House, Linktown in 1728 and lies buried in Westminster Abbey. He was renowned for his attention to detail and his architectural masterpieces include Register House and Edinburgh University in Scotland, and over the border he made a major contribution to Georgian London.

George Gillespie was born in 1613 and became the youngest ever Moderator to the General Assembly of the Church of Scotland. He wrote a controversial book about English Popish Ceremonies which was not well received by the authorities. The book was subsequently burned by the hangman in Edinburgh. After a very promising start to his career Gillespie died in 1647, age 34.

John Ritchie was born in 1778 and established a reputation as a successful merchant in Edinburgh in the early 1800's. In 1831 he took over the management of The Scotsman newspaper.

Marjory Fleming (1803-1812) was a remarkable young girl whose poetry was widely acclaimed. Her diaries also attracted great interest as they gave a detailed account of her life and the major events of the time. She was buried in Abbotshall Kirkyard.

Sir Sandford Fleming was born in 1827 in Glasswork Street. He invented the International Date Line which was accepted as Standard Time in 1883 and he was the chief engineer in charge of laying the Canadian Pacific Railway.

Michael Scott (about 1115-1234) was born in Balwearie Castle and studied at Oxford and Paris. He was appointed official astrologer at the court of Frederick II. His extensive knowledge of mathematics and medicine gave him an aura of mystique, which in those superstitious days was associated with magic, hence his nickname The Wizard of the North. Perhaps the Wizards greatest feat was to rid Kirkcaldy of the Devil. Legend tells us that the Wizard challenged the Devil to make a rope out of the sand at Kirkcaldy harbour. This proved totally beyond the Devil and he disappeared forever.

The last duel in Fife involved two Kirkcaldy men. David Landale, a merchant, challenged George Morgan, an agent for the Bank of Scotland, to a duel. They met on the 23rd August, 1826 in a field near Auchterderran, and Morgan fell mortally wounded. At the subsequent trial in Perth a clever defence ensured that Landale was found not guilty.

When Andrew Wilson of Pathhead was hung in Edinburgh in 1736 the crowd rioted and this led to the infamous Porteous riots. John Buchan spent his youth in Pathhead and the '39 Steps' in his novel supposedly lead from Ravenscraig Castle to the beach. The Castle was built on the orders of James II to defend Fife and the Firth of Forth. James III granted the Castle to the Sinclairs of Orkney who held ownership till 1896. It is now maintained by the State and is an impressive ruin overlooking the Forth.

Parish Church, Kirk Wynd.

Old Kirkcaldy has since long vanished and with it a lot of the character. There are, however, individual buildings of note which have survived and they include Dunnikier House - now Path House, Sailors Walk and the Parish Church. Old Dunnikier House commands a splendid view of Kirkcaldy esplanade and the Firth of Forth from its well chosen site at Pathhead. Built in 1692 by John Watson it was later owned by the Oswald family of Dunnikier. The House has had several owners and uses since then, and in 1979 it was given an amenity award by Kirkcaldy Civic Society.

Overlooking the harbour are the distinctive crow stepped gables of Sailors Walk which was built about the mid-15th century and is now the oldest building in Kirkcaldy. It was restored between 1954-59 and is owned by the National Trust for Scotland, and used as the Customs House.

Dominating Kirk Wynd is the old Parish Church which was consecrated in 1244 and is now the oldest Church in the Kirkcaldy area. The tower dates back to about 1500 with the body of the Kirk built in 1808. In the shadow of the Church stands a quaint old house built in 1637 for a local corn merchant. The lodging house at 22, Kirk Wynd was the home of Thomas Carlyle, the author and schoolmaster, who stayed in Kirkcaldy between 1816-18 when he was the Master of Kirkcaldy Burgh School.

The Town House is the headquarters of Kirkcaldy District Council. It replaced the old Town Hall that was situated in Tolbooth Street and demolished in 1953. A competition was held for the design of the new Town House in 1937. The winning design began on site in 1939 but was not finally completed until 1956 due to the disruption of the Second World War. Inside, a mural by Walter Pritchard depicts the industrial history of Kirkcaldy along with the famous people associated with the town. Standing on top of the Town House is an unusual weathervane. The figure is that of St. Bryce, the Patron Saint of Kirkcaldy. The Provost's Lamps outside the Town House are a reminder of the days of the old Burgh Councils before local government reorganisation.

Kirkcaldy has undergone much demolition since the 1960's and new facilities such as a pedestrian High Street, shopping centre, swimming pool and car parks have done much to improve the amenities of the town. The railway station was rebuilt in 1992 after a fire gutted the station built in 1964. This had replaced the original station built in 1847 - a year after the railway arrived in Kirkcaldy. Nearby is the Art Gallery, Museum and Public Library complex. The Museum has an excellent display on industrial Kirkcaldy featuring linoleum and other local industries such as the Wemyss Ware pottery. One event which is still thriving is the ever popular Links Market. It started in 1304 and every Eastertime the long esplanade is closed off for what is recognised as Europe's largest street fair.

Town Hall, Kirkcaldy.

17

The Clock Shop, Thornton.

Thornton would originally have been a scattered farming community and a bridging point as it is sandwiched between the Rivers Ore and Lochty. It is likely that Thornton gained its name from the marriage of Lord Balgonie to a Miss Thornton from London in 1879. By the 19th century a combination of coal mining, weaving and the arrival of the railway had turned Thornton into a thriving community. Coal had most likely been mined from near the surface as early as the 13th century and by the 19th century the four main pits in the area were the Balgonie, Julian, Lochty and Randolph. The coal from these pits was used to generate steam power for the industries located along the Ore and Lochty. Situated so close to the rivers Thornton was an ideal site for the mills which established the village as a small weaving centre. This attracted associated industries such as the Bleachfields which set up nearby, and operated until 1883.

The arrival of the railway line in 1847, which then linked Kirkcaldy with Dundee, plus the building of the railway sidings established Thornton as a major railway junction in the area. The decline of both coal and weaving industries and later, the closure of the railway junction in 1969 badly affected Thornton. False hope of a spirited recovery was kindled by the building of the Rothes Colliery in the 1950's. A cruel combination of continual flooding and difficulty in extracting the coal forced the National Coal Board to close the pit in 1961 at a cost of £14 million.

The construction of the new Kirkcaldy – Glenrothes road in 1981 by-passed Thornton thus relieving the village of an acute traffic problem. But in spite of Thornton becoming a backwater it still attracts enthusiasts for the greyhound racing at the local track which was built in 1930; the Highland Games held annually in July and the 18 hole golf course which was founded in 1921.

Famous people from Thornton include James Black who copied Thomas Jefferson's draft of the American Declaration of Independence. Black was chosen because of his neat hand-writing and this draft was based on the theories of another Fifer, James Wilson, who emigrated to North America in 1765.

The most famous Fifer who was associated with Thornton was David Hatton who was born in 1784 in Dunfermline. He was renowned for his inventions and the most successful was the 'Fluotorum' - a new type of Flute. Eventually he settled in Thornton and made a living by charging people to see him lying in his coffin. Hatton also invented a contraption to wind cotton threads onto spools, which were driven by mice running on a treadmill. Not surprisingly, there were no sponsors interested in financing this invention on a commercial scale. Hatton died in 1851 and was buried in Dysart. He is not forgotten, however, as Hatton Avenue in Thornton is named after him.

The Rothes Colliery, Thornton. The above winding towers were demolished on 14th March, 1993.

'The Dream'

Glenrothes was founded under the New Towns Act of 1946 and the Glenrothes Development Corporation was then formed in 1948 to plan and control the development of this New Town. The GDC was to be responsible for generating economic growth and to ensure that Glenrothes developed as a well balanced and integrated community. The Planners had virtually a free hand as the site only included the two small villages of Cadham and Woodside. Consequently a Town Centre with shops and offices was to form the nucleus of the New Town with residential areas grouped around this centre. The increasing importance of the motor car influenced the design of these residential areas which have a good road network that links with the main Kirkcaldy – Dundee road. Good communications were vital to attract business and Glenrothes' location is ideally situated for linking up with the major road, rail, sea and air routes.

Initially the Rothes Pit near Thornton was to be one of the main industries but its unexpected closure in 1961 changed the Planners priorities. At this time it was intended that Glenrothes cope with the population overspill from Glasgow. Therefore plans were formed to develop Glenrothes as a manufacturing centre which would attract industrial investment.

In 1958 the First new firm to put roots down in Glenrothes was Beckman Instruments at Queensway Industrial Estate. Since then Glenrothes has expanded into a major micro-electronics centre in Scotland and many firms have chosen Glenrothes as an industrial base. Major firms have contributed to this successful development and they include Hughes Microelectronics, Alma Confectionery, Velux and Canon. With the reorganisation of local government in 1975 Glenrothes has developed as the administrative centre of the Fife Region and Fife Regional Council has established its headquarters in the Town Centre.

In 1968 a Town Artist was appointed and the many sculptures and brick or concrete murals are now an integral part of the town design. Concrete hippos, totem poles, a giant hand and toadstools are just some of the sculptures which add a sense of identity and fun to the landscaped open spaces. The bronze sculpture of the dancing children, designed by the present Town Artist, Malcolm Robertson, was created for Böblingen in Germany which is the twin town of Glenrothes. A replica stands near the town centre and the dancing children represent 'The Dream' - the unity of people of mixed ethnic backgrounds.

The GDC has achieved its goal of establishing Glenrothes as a successful community with good facilities and a sound industrial base. Consequently the GDC will be wound up in 1994 now that the infrastructure is in place for continued development.

Nestling down by the River Leven in the shadow of Cadham are the Tullis Russell Paper Mills founded in 1809. Tullis Russell is the largest independently owned paper manufacturer in the U.K. Within this complex there are three paper mills producing approximately 70,000 tonnes of paper and board each year. Tullis Russell also pioneered the Twin Wire Process of papermaking and operate the largest TruFlo Coating Plant in the world. Their products are not only distributed throughout the U.K. but are exported to a worldwide market.

GDC Coat of Arms - 'Out of Earth-Strength'

Kirk·on·the·Green, Leslie.

Leslie was known as Fettykil until 1283 when Alexander III made a grant of the lands and woods of Fettykil to Norman de Leslie. The village was created a Burgh of Barony in 1458 and the green at the east end of the High Street has long been a scene of village fairs and sport. The Church overlooks the green and there are serious claims that it was Leslie which featured in the old poem 'Christ's Kirk on the Green' - possibly written by James I or V. Leslie was the headquarters for the packmen of Scotland and the Packmen's Fairs were a time of great festivity and merrymaking at the green. One of the more barbaric but popular sports was bullbaiting and the boulder near the Church gates is known as the Bull Stone. The groove around the stone held the rope which tethered the bulls while they tried to fend off the attacking bulldogs. This cruel 'sport' was abolished in 1835. The present Church on the green was built in 1821, then extended in 1869, and replaced an earlier church founded in 1591.

Leslie House was built for the 7th Earl of Rothes in 1667-72 and was intended to rival the Palace of Holyroodhouse. A disastrous fire in 1763 burned down three wings resulting in a major reconstruction in 1767. Today the house is a Church of Scotland home. Like many other Fife villages Leslie benefitted from the upsurge in the weaving industry in the 1800's. Situated by the River Leven it was ideally placed for the flax mills and then latterly the paper mills.

The Romans named the mountain tribes north of the Forth and Clyde as the 'Picti' - the painted ones.' Markinch was reputedly the ancient capital of these Picts who aggressively defended Ancient Caledonia against repeated Roman invasion. It was the Scots led by Kenneth MacAlpin, however, who finally subdued the Picts in the 9th century. Once defeated the Picts and their culture simply disappeared. All that remains today are mysterious standing stones and carvings on cave walls or stone slabs - but nothing exists to explain the Pictish laws, legends or religion. They are a lost race and a puzzle that remains unsolved.

St. Drostan, a nephew of St. Columba, is the Patron Saint of Markinch. The tall tower of St. Drostan's Church, standing high on Markinch Hill dates back to about 1200. The Church was rebuilt in 1786 and buried inside is the famous General, Sir Alexander Leslie who died at Balgonie Castle in 1661. An ancient stone slab with a carved cross stands on the north side of Markinch. This is the Stob Cross which was one of several old Girth stones that marked the boundaries of a Sanctuary as established by the Church. Another landmark is the railway viaduct and nearby stands the red brick building of John Haig & Co., the famous whisky blenders. This building is now used as the offices of the Glenrothes Development Corporation. At one time the GDC occupied Balbirnie House which was built in 1777. It is now a Hotel and the grounds contain the Balbirnie Craft Centre, a golf course, caravan park and an ancient stone circle dating back to the Bronze Age.

St. Drostan's Church, Markinch.

East Quality Street, Dysart.

Dysart was an independent burgh until 1929 when it amalgamated with Kirkcaldy. The Dysart Town Hall and Tolbooth, however, still survive amidst the new housing schemes of the 1960's when the heart of old Dysart was torn out and redeveloped. The Town Hall was built in 1887 to replace an older building of 1617. The Tolbooth is much older dating back to 1576 and used to house the Public Weigh-House, Prison, Guard-house and the Black Hole. In 1656 when Cromwell's troops occupied the town a drunken soldier accidently dropped a burning torch into a barrell of gunpowder. The resultant explosion severely damaged the roof and building which stood in ruins for several years before they were repaired. Standing on the site of the old Mercat Cross outside the Tolbooth is an ornamental lamp which was erected in 1887 to commemorate the Golden Jubilee of Queen Victoria's reign.

Dysart was the birthplace in 1815 of John McDouall Stuart, the Australian explorer. The house still stands today, tucked in behind Normand Hall, and contains a museum of his exploits in Australia. After studying as a Civil Engineer, Stuart emigrated to Australia in 1838. From 1844 onwards he set off on a series of expeditions into unknown territory. In 1860 he discovered the centre of Australia and after five unsuccessful attempts to cross Australia from south to north he finally succeeded in 1862. This was the first ever desert crossing and the Stuart Highway from Alice Springs to Darwin and Mount Stuart in central Australia are named after him.

A local saying "As old as the three trees of Dysart" implies that this is an ancient town. Indeed Dysart takes its name from the old legend of St. Serf who lived in a cave or 'deserta' - a religious retreat in the grounds of the nearby Carmelite Monastery. It was here that St. Serf wrestled with Auld Nick, the devil and succeeded in banishing him from this area.

Dysart blossomed as a prosperous port and was founded as a Burgh of Barony in 1510 with Lord Sinclair, the feudal superior. The Sinclairs trace their family back to the great Barons of Normandy about 1000 A.D. On reaching this country the Sinclairs eventually became Earls of Orkney and therefore vassals of the Crown of Norway. In 1476 James III married Margaret of Denmark and both Orkney and Shetland were annexed to the Scottish Crown. James then ordered William Sinclair to exchange the Earldom of Orkney for the estates of Dysart and Ravensheugh. The Sinclairs held great sway in the area until the death of William Sinclair in 1840 when his estates were all divided up.

For many years Dysart was known as 'Little Holland' due to its trade with the Low Countries and the import of Dutch tiles which were used on the houses. It was also named the 'Saut Burgh' because of its flourishing salt industry which produced the salt necessary to preserve the fish for export. The salt pans were at Pan Ha' near the shore and this airt of Dysart was renovated by the National Trust for Scotland in 1969.

Tolbooth, Dysart.

25

The Bay House and St. Serf's Tower, Dysart.

Pan Ha' or Pan Haugh includes many fine 16th to 18th century houses especially the Anchorage at the top of the Hie Gate. To the west of Pan Ha' is the Bay House, built in 1583 for the Sinclair Family. Carved into the skewputts at each corner are the faces of James VI, Queen Ann and their son Charles. Nearby is the 16th century 80 foot high tower of St. Serfs Church. This is virtually all that remains of the Church after it was abandoned in 1802 and then demolished for the building of Shore Road.

Up until the 18th century Dysart was a thriving industrial area with the salt, mining, shipbuilding, linen and nail industries all benefiting from the port facilities allowing trade with England and the Low Countries. Each year in April, June and October eight day markets were held for the sale of local goods which were only sold at these markets at a price fixed by the Council. From 1750 onwards the weaving industry was booming and the demand for linen far **exceeded** supply. In order to cope Dysart farmed out work to other Fife villages at Ladybank, Ceres and Strathmiglo. Around 1800 the introduction of English woolcloth and replacement of the hand loom with the power loom led to a drastic fall in demand and with it the decline of the Dysart linen industry.

26

One man who kept pace with the winds of change was James Normand. He supervised the changeover from the hand loom to the power loom and established linen and flax mills in Dysart which employed up to 500 people. In 1885 the Normand Memorial Hall was built and donated to the people of Dysart by his widow. Another industry that was long associated with Dysart was the nail industry and in the 18th century no less than 100 smithies were involved in producing nails.

Dysart harbour dates from the early 17th century and replaced the old pier at Pan Ha' which had fallen into decay and had silted up by 1615. Further expansion took place in 1831 when a wet dock was created out of a quarry to cope with the increase in trade and shipbuilding. Not all industries were booming, however, and the early 1800's saw the linen and salt industries start to decline. By 1900 the export of coal and shipbuilding activities had dwindled rapidly and business was lost to the larger ports of Methil and Burntisland which offered more modern facilities. The closure of the local Lady Blanche Colliery in 1928 effectively sealed the fate of Dysart harbour and it was closed as a commercial port in 1929.

Marriage lintel over doorway in the Hie Gate, Pan Ha.

Hie Gate, Pan Ha'.   27

Macduff Castle, East Wemyss.

The three Wemyss villages of Coaltown of Wemyss, East Wemyss and West Wemyss are located around Macduff Castle and Wemyss Castle. The original timber stronghold was Macduff Castle which was named after Macduff, Thane of Fife. Macduff claimed descent from a son of Eochaid the Fair, a 7th century King of the Picts, and the Macduff Clan ruled their province as a Kingdom until the beginning of the 12th century. They also held the hereditary right to crown the King of Scots. In the 11th century King Macbeth imprisoned Macduff at the Castle but he luckily escaped and made his way across the border to England. Macduff eventually returned to defeat Macbeth in battle in Aberdeenshire in 1057 - far from Birnam Wood and Dunsinane as dramatised by Shakespeare.

The Wemyss family are descended from Macduff and it was Sir John of Methil and Wemyss who adopted the Wemyss surname in the early 13th century. It is possible that he instructed the building of the first stone castle which was raised to the ground by Edward 1 of England in 1306. It was rebuilt and remained occupied until the 17th century. In 1666 it was recorded that the Countess of Sutherland, a daughter of the 2nd Earl of Wemyss, stayed here with her family to escape the plague which was affecting Edinburgh. The bid for safety failed and thereafter the Castle fell into ruin and only the remains of one tower are standing today.

Wemyss Castle was built in the early 15th century when the Wemyss family sold Macduff Castle. Built right on the edge of the cliffs Wemyss Castle has a commanding view out over the Firth of Forth. The Castle has been modified and extended many times over the centuries and has hosted Royalty on more than one occasion. In 1565, it was here that Mary Queen of Scots met and fell in love with Lord Darnley, who soon after became her husband. Other Royal visitors were James VI and then Charles II who toured Fife in 1650.

The village of East Wemyss grew up around the Castle and from the 12th century onwards East Wemyss was associated with the weaving industry. This reached its peak in the 16th and 17th century with linen exported to a ready market in England and on the continent. The local hand looms all established a good business, but then large hand loom factories and the introduction of the powerloom, forced the small weavers out of business. In order to compete the local firm James and George Johnson opened a power loom factory in 1860 and soon they had 200 steam powered looms producing linen. The firm is now Wemyss Weavecraft Ltd and concentrates on producing furnishing fabrics. The Wemyss area is rich in history and the Wemyss Environmental Education Centre provides detailed information to schools on all aspects of local interest.

Macduff - Thane of Fife

Michael Colliery Memorial, East Wemyss.

At the end of the 19th century coalmining replaced weaving as the main industry. The Rosie Pit was opened in 1886 and then the Michael Colliery in 1898 which was named after Captain Michael Wemyss of Wemyss Castle. The Michael Colliery allowed access to the Dysart Main Seam which was recognised as an unstable coal liable to spontaneous combustion. This caused a disastrous underground fire at the Colliery in 1967. Nine men lost their lives and the pit shafts had to be sealed off. The pit closure was a cruel blow to the local economy.

In 1977 the National Coal Board made arrangements to extract coal from the Michael Colliery by linking it with the Frances and Seafield Collieries. Today a memorial of a winding wheel stands appropriately at the approach to the disused Michael Colliery in Miners Row. This commemorates the nine men who tragically died in the fire and stands as a reminder to a village that was once a thriving mining community. Miners Row was built by the Wemyss Coal Company in 1900 as homes for the miners and the cottages are now included within the conservation area.

The oldest Church in the village was St. Mary's by-the-sea dating back to the reign of David I (1124-53). It was rebuilt in 1528, with improvements in the 1790's but in 1976 was closed down. Since then it has been used as a private home and a recording studio.

The coastal village of West Wemyss was established around Wemyss Castle and was made a Burgh of Barony by James IV in 1511. Initially salt making was the main industry but this was gradually replaced by coal mining in the mid 19th century. West Wemyss was suitably close to several coal mines and consequently established a thriving trade by exporting coal to England and the Low Countries. In spite of improved harbour facilities West Wemyss could not compete with the new docks at Methil. By the end of the 19th century coal exports started to decline rapidly and the harbour soon fell into decay.

The village has now been designated a Conservation Area and has several interesting buildings. These include the Tolbooth in the Main Street which has a panel of the Wemyss Coat of Arms on the front wall. The swans incorporated into the Coat of Arms represent a learned person and appropriately the Wemyss motto is 'Je pense' – 'I think.' Further along the street stands the old Miners Institute which closed in 1952 but has been successfully converted into a hotel.

To the west of the village stands the Chapel, reputedly built by Spaniards who sought refuge here from the Spanish Inquisition in the 15th century. A circular tower in the boundary wall was originally used as a doocot and the chapel grounds contain the Wemyss family burial ground.

Tolbooth, West Wemyss.

31

West Wemyss

Wemyss is a derivation of 'weems' which is based on the Gaelic word 'uamh' meaning a cave. This refers to a series of caves near Macduff Castle which were formed between 3000 and 7000 years B.C. The caves have been used since those early days by Picts, Christian missionaries and Norsemen. They also contain more ancient inscriptions and drawings on the walls than all the other caves in Britain. The oldest drawings date back to the Bronze Age 4000 years B.C. and although there used to be twelve known caves only five exist today.

Jonathon's Cave contains more markings than all the other caves with drawings of elephants, boats, fish, horses, dogs and swans - the latter was chosen as the crest of the Wemyss family. The cave is also known as the Factors Cave because it was here that the local folk of East Wemyss came to pay their rates.

The Well Cave refers to the existence of a well and its clear water was supposed to cure illness. In Pictish times a well was an object of worship as it was the source of water. Perhaps this explains a 'Hansel Monday' custom by the folk of East Wemyss. After 1752 the first Monday after the 11th of January was marked with a torchlit procession to the cave. Then as part of an ancient custom the water from the well was drunk amidst great scenes of celebration, singing and feasting.

When Christianity was introduced to Scotland this well was later named after St. Margaret - the Queen of Malcolm Canmore in the 11th century. The Well Cave was sometimes known as Castle Cave as a secret passage led to the Castle above.

The Court Cave refers to the days in the 15th to 17th century when the Baron Courts were held here by the owners of Macduff Castle. Local legend also tells of the time when James V, disguised as the Guidman of Ballengeich made the acquaintance of some gypsies sheltering in the cave. After a while trouble broke out and James revealed his true identity to command obedience. The gypsies were stunned that a King should seek their company and treated him with the utmost respect. The Court Cave is haunted by the White Lady - a local lass who was wrongly convicted of stealing and later died brokenhearted in the cave. For centuries the White Lady has made fleeting appearances near the caves - perhaps to haunt the gypsies associated with her demise.

In 1610 George Hay built one of the first glassmaking factories in Scotland in what was known as the Glass Cave. Other caves include the Gasworks Cave, the Sliding Cave and the Doo Cave, each with their own history dating back thousands of years. The Caves are a part of our ancient heritage and surely deserve a better fate than the vandalism and neglect that has occurred there over many years.

Main Street, Coaltown of Wemyss.

33

Coronation Place, Coaltown of Wemyss.

Coaltown of Wemyss is situated inland at the entrance to Wemyss Castle and derives its name from the old 'Bell-shaped' Pits in the area. Originally there were two small villages-Easter and Wester Coaltown which also provided accommodation for the agricultural workers on the Wemyss Estate. The expansion of the coal industry in the 19th century resulted in the Wemyss Coal Company building cottages for the incoming miners and the two villages merged into one. Even today the old cottages in South Row, Barns Place, Coronation Place and Main Street still capture the character of the old mining village. Consequently Kirkcaldy District Council have declared all the old streets a conservation area. This is a policy that they pursue, where appropriate throughout the area.

At the east end of the village stands the Earl David Hotel, built in 1911 by Lady Eva Wemyss. It was initially known as Coaltown of Wemyss Public House Society and the profits were ploughed back into developing the community. The idea was based on a Swedish system and the row of houses alongside the hotel are known as Gothenburg Terrace in recognition of this. Later the hotel was named Earl David after the 4th Earl of Wemyss (1705-1720). The family motto, shown on the next page, is carved into an elaborate lintel over the main door.

JE PENSE

The Wemyss School of Needlework was set up by Lady Dorothy Wemyss at Wemyss Castle in 1877. Shortly after 1880 the school moved to its present location in Main Street at the entrance to Wemyss Castle. It provided training for young girls in the art of needlework and embroidery and today is involved in the repairs of old tapestries and fabric.

At the west end of the village guarding the road down to West Wemyss is the Bowhouse Tollhouse built initially in 1800 then rebuilt in 1906. Its distinctive octagon shape allowed an all round view of the countryside. This allowed travellers to be seen approaching from any direction and no doubt ensured that they paid the road toll down to West Wemyss.

Bowhouse Tollhouse

35

Swan Insignia

Folklore tells of a Dutch vessel that was shipwrecked in the Firth of Forth about 1500. The survivors built a settlement around a natural harbour at the foot of the slopes. This became the village of Buckhyne - the roaring harbour - which clung precariously to its narrow foothold on the rocky shore. Buckhyne, now known as Buckhaven, was initially a close knit fishing community. Eventually most folk were either named Thomson or related to one and this spawned the familiar saying "We're all Jock Tamson's bairns."

In 1831 Buckhaven boasted 198 boats and formed the second largest fishing fleet in Scotland behind Buckie. In order to cope with this large fleet the harbour was extended in 1838 and again in 1849. Buckhaven continued to flourish with both fishing and weaving providing gainful employment but by 1880 both industries had slipped into a slow decline. The coal industry, however, helped to revitalise Buckhaven. In 1864 Bowman & Co. had reopened the Muiredge Colliery and then in the 1870's had opened the Denbeath mine.

The railway arrived at Buckhaven in 1881 and was extended to link up with Methil No 1 dock in 1887. As happened throughout this airt of Fife the development of Methil docks as the main port greatly affected other harbours along this east coast. Only Burntisland docks and harbour expanded sufficiently to compete with Methil.

Old Provost's Lamp, Buckhaven & Methil.

Consequently plans to develop Buckhaven harbour were shelved in 1905. Thereafter deposits of redd from the mines slowly silted up the harbour. With the fishing industry virtually gone folk left the overcrowded harbour area which quickly fell into decay. In the 1960's Auld Buckhyne was demolished and the new housing scheme along the shore has scarcely recaptured the character of the old fishing village.

Of particular note in Buckhaven is the Free Church which originally stood in North Street, St. Andrews. In 1890 it was bought by the Free Kirk and transported stone by stone round the coast to its present site. With regards to education the Church of Scotland established an Adventure School at Buckhaven in 1810. This closed in 1885 when the Madras School at Braehead opened and by 1895 the School was the first in Scotland to be recognised as a Higher Grade Public School. In 1958 the new Buckhaven High School was opened at Methilhaven Road and the old school, which closed in 1971, was renamed Braehead Secondary School.

Today Buckhaven relies heavily on the oil construction yards on the site of the old Denbeath mine. The Wemyss Coal Co. took over the mine, in 1905 and renamed it the Wellesley Colliery. This closed in 1967 and Redpath Dorman took over the site in 1972 for oil construction yards. In 1978 the Dutch took over and the company was renamed RGC - Redpath de Groot Cale.

Randolph Wemyss Memorial Hospital, Buckhaven. 37

High Street, Methil.

Initially 'Methkil' was controlled by the Cathedral of St. Andrews but a charter of 1215 specifically refers to Methil as a separate estate from the nearby Kirklands. This estate was owned by John, son of Michael of Methil, who was later knighted as Sir John of Methil and Wemyss. He was a distant descendant of Macduff, the Thane of Fife, who founded the Wemyss family in the reign of Malcolm IV.

Methil has an industrial history dating back to the days of the early charters. In 1660 permission was granted from Charles I to build a harbour at Methil. This was vital for the easy import and export of goods and materials in an area where the coal, salt and fishing industries were steadily expanding. The success of this industrial development is simply acknowledged in the motto which Methil adopted – 'Carbon Carbasque' – 'by coal and by sail'. They were the two factors which put Methil on the industrial map. The salt industry, however, was dealt a harsh blow in 1825 with the imposition of a salt tax. This effectively forced the closure of the salt pans as the duty due to the Government became too exhorbitant. The coal industry continued to prosper and between 1870 and 1880 coal output in Fife had doubled. In order to cope with this demand a new dock was constructed in 1883 and in conjunction with a new rail link from Thornton Junction, Methil became the biggest port in this part of the country by the early 1900's.

The building of another two docks by 1913 increased Methil's importance to the detriment of other major ports such as Burntisland. After the Second World War Methil Docks declined in activity and the closure of both the Wellesley Colliery and Michael Colliery in 1967 greatly affected its livelihood. Since then Methil has undergone massive changes with vast areas demolished to make way for new developments. In the 1970's No 3 dock was closed and the Scottish Development Agency converted the area into an industrial estate to attract industry and further investment back into the area. In 1963 the Methil Power Station was built at the mouth of the River Leven and forms a towering landmark on the east coast.

In the 1920's a local firm, Moncrieff Electrical Contractors, were pioneers in the production of washing machines. It was named the Moncrieff Thistle and had a knife sharpener and polisher attached to the wringer. The machines were manufactured in Suttie Street, Methil and exported all over the world.

Finally a mention of Methil would not be complete without reference to East Fife, the local football team who play at Bayview. They were formed in 1910 and are the only Second Division Club to win the Scottish Cup. This happened in 1938 and further success followed in 1947, '49 and '53 when they won the Scottish League Cup.

Wellesley Road, Buckhaven

The Greig Institute, Leven

Leven falls within the ancient Parish of Scoonie which was first granted to the Culdees of Loch Leven in the early 11th century. In 1152 the Parish was then granted to the Priory of St. Andrews and the old Scoonie Church was later consecrated in 1243. Early settlement, however, concentrated around the harbour at the mouth of the River Leven. The name Leven is of Pictish origin meaning flood and no doubt Loch Leven - the flood lake - gave its name to both the river and town.

In 1609 Leven was made a Burgh of Barony, and by the late 1700's there was a sound industrial base with a bleachworks, a rope factory, weaving and a harbour which catered for a small fishing fleet. In 1808 the Durie Foundry was built on the old bleachwork site. Henry Balfour and James Anderson of Dundee later bought the foundry and established it as one of the leading manufacturers in gaswork apparatus and industrial components. In 1879 a new dock was built but this was of short benefit to Leven as the North British Railway Company bought both Methil and Leven docks in 1886 and chose to develop Methil docks. Consequently the Leven harbour soon silted up and was completely filled in by 1910. Communications improved at the turn of the century and the Bawbee Brig was built in 1907. This was replaced by the present bridge in 1957. A bawbee or ha'penny had always been charged for the ferry crossing and this toll continued when a footbridge was built in 1821. The toll was abolished in 1870 but the name Bawbee Brig still remains today.

During the late 1800's the railway and then the tram link to Gallatown in 1906 helped to establish Leven as a tourist resort. Golf was one of the main attractions and the Leven Golfing Society, which was an amalgamation of two local clubs in 1957, can claim to be the twelfth oldest club in the world. The L.G.S. is an amalgamation of the Innerleven Golfing Club founded in 1820 and the Leven Golf Club founded in 1877. The Innerleven G.S. originally played at Dubbieside, now the site of Methil Power Station but in 1867 they decided to play on Leven Links. The same year Leven Thistle Golf Club was formed and today the Thistle Club and Golfing Society still use the same links although each Club has its own Clubhouse.

The famous Nicoll Cleek making firm set up in 1881 and was associated with Henry Cotton in the design and manufacture of clubs until it closed in 1984. The other local golf club manufacturer was JR Carstairs which was later taken over by Bob Harrison but this firm has closed down recently. An unusual tourist attraction was artistically created by William Bissett who decorated his own house, garden walls and an old bus with sea shells, China and coloured glass. It became very popular with tourists and was known as the Buckie House. In 1891 the old Leven Mercat Cross was discovered in the walls of the Greig Institute. It now stands in the grounds of Carberry House which was presented to Leven in 1929 by Sir Robert Balfour as a memorial to his brother.

Leven Thistle Golf Clubhouse with the Leven Golfing Society Clubhouse in the background. 41

Balgonie Castle

Balgonie Castle stands proudly between the villages of Milton of Balgonie and Coaltown of Balgonie. The Castle was built about 1360 by Sir Thomas Sibbald of Balgonie with a defensive ditch around three sides and the other side protected by the steep bank to the River Leven. The Castle was continually modified and changed owners many times before it was bought by the famous soldier and General - Sir Alexander Leslie. During the Thirty Years War Leslie was appointed by King Gustav of Sweden as Field Marshall to the Swedish army. By 1638, however, Leslie was back in Scotland as leader of the Protestant army of the Solemn League and Covenant which easily captured Edinburgh Castle in 1639. Two years later Leslie was made 1st Earl of Leven and Lord Balgonie. In 1651 he was captured at Alyth by General Monk and imprisoned in the Tower of London. Luckily the Queen of Sweden made a special plea on his behalf and he was released in 1654. On his return to Balgonie Castle he added the top floor to the north range and replaced the great oak trees which had been cut down to provide the roof beams at the Parliament Hall in Edinburgh. Leslie died in 1661 and was buried in Markinch Church. In 1716 Rob Roy MacGregor temporarily occupied the Castle after capturing it from the Hanoverian forces. In the early 1800's the Castle was abandoned and lay in ruins until it was partially restored in 1971. The Castle was then bought in 1985 by the present Laird - Raymond Morris of Balgonie and Eddergoll who intends to complete the restoration work. The Chapel and 14th century Great Hall are popular for weddings and the Castle is open to the public all year round.

Downstream from Balgonie Castle is Milton of Balgonie. As the name implies the livelihood of this village depended on the mills located on the River Leven. The Balgonie Flax mill was built in 1806 by William Drummond. The Flax was spun into yarn or thread at the mill and then distributed to the cottage weavers throughout Fife to be woven into linen. Like many other industrial ventures the mill hit hard times and became bankrupt in 1810. It was eventually rescued by Robert Baxter and Joseph Gordon Stuart who founded the successful firm Baxter and Stuarts. By 1840 about 260 people were working at the mill which operated 100 looms to produce heavy yarn for weaving into canvas which was then exported to London. Building on this success the firm expanded the business and Baxter established the first spinning mills in Lille, France in 1843. Ironically, by the 1880's, it was cheaper yarn imported from Europe which signalled the decline of the Flax industry in Fife and by 1886 the mill was closed down.

The Balfour Family owned land in the Balgonie area from the time of King Duncan in 1040 and in the mid-18th century Balfour House was built on the estates. By the 1930's the house lay in ruins and a copse now marks the site. The most famous Balfour of national fame was Arthur James Balfour (1848-1930) who was Prime Minister of the Unionist Party from 1902-1905.

Milton of Balgonie Parish Church

Coaltown of Balgonie

Coaltown of Balgonie owed its existence to the coal industry. It is probable that coal was extracted from 'Bell Pits' as early as the 13th century. These were simply vertical shafts sunk to the level of the coal seam where the shaft was enlarged or belled out to extract the coal. With the River Leven so close, flooding was always a problem in the pits. Consequently in 1731 the 'Earls of Leven and Melville built 'Balgonie Engines' - a water pump located in a house to the west of the Castle. The coal mines were run by the Landale brothers who built a windmill in 1732 to also help with water pumping - but to no avail and the mines closed in 1743. Much later, in 1785 the mines reopened and in 1921 the Balgonie Coal Company built a weir and turbine on the River Leven to provide power for the nearby pits. In 1947 the Company was nationalised and both the mines and turbines were finally closed down in 1960. Tullis Russell, the local paper manufacturer, bought the power station in 1981 and restored it to working order for the benefits of the paper mill.

Another local industry associated with coal was the ironworks. It started in 1800 with the formation of Leven Coal Company. The venture floundered in 1803 when the Company went bankrupt, although it reopened in 1805 before finally closing down in 1814. At its peak the ironworks had provided employment for 490 people. The hall opposite was presented by C.B. Balfour MP and opened in 1906.

North of Windygates lies the village of Kennoway - one of the oldest settlements in Fife. In olden times, probably about the 7th century, St. Cainnech founded a retreat here and set up an early Culdee Church close to the ancient Maiden Castle. This Castle would have been a very old Pictish fort built of timber and sitting atop a mound for defence. In 1619 the first substantial Parish Church was built in the Causeway but this was abandoned in 1849. A new site was chosen for the new Church which claims the oldest Communion Cup in Scotland dating back to 1651. Up until 1750 Kennoway had a small brewery but when this closed down the village became a backwater.

The arrival of the weaving industry in the late 18th century rejuvenated Kennoway and many of the old weavers cottages still survive today. Naturally enough when the weaving industry petered out, towards the end of the 19th century, Kennoway went into decline. The population was expanded in the 1930's and again in the 1950's when new housing estates were built to accommodate mining families from Ayrshire. The Den in Kennoway once had a bleachfield and hollowed out in the sandstone rock are two small caves. They were reputedly a hiding place of John Knox, the Reformer, and perhaps there is a secret tunnel leading down to Windygates! Seton House in the Causeway was where Archbishop Sharp spent his last night before being ambushed and cruelly murdered by the Covenanters in 1679.

Parish Church, Kennoway.

45

In the days of stagecoach travel Windygates was the busy posting station in East Fife. The cross-roads linked the roads from North, East and Central Fife with the road south to the ferry port of Pettycur on the Firth of Forth. A tollhouse and tollgate stood at the cross and all horse drawn carriages had to pay a toll there until 1907. Today the main Kirkcaldy - Leven road and Glenrothes - Leven road by pass Windygates. Opposite the early 19th century Windygates Hotel stands a cast iron clock dated 1916 with a plaque stating 'Erected from the Proceeds of Social Betterment Dairy Scheme'. The clock was erected as a memorial to the scheme which was to encourage the drinking of milk instead of alcohol. The reason for this was the Government's concern that overindulgence in alcohol was disrupting the war effort.

The Windygates Clock

Cameron Bridge was initially a small weaving and mining community but is now renowned for its connection with whisky. The first distillery was run by Robert Haig and John Eddington from about 1813 to 1817 then it was bought over by John Haig in 1818. The distillery produced a lowland malt whisky but when the Corn Laws were relaxed it concentrated on the production of grain whisky. In fact the distillery is renowned for its own distinctive single grain whisky - Cameron Brig. In 1877 Cameron Bridge distillery amalgamated with five other grain whisky distilleries to form D.C.L. - the Distillers Company Limited. It was then that the Haig family whisky merchanting business, which had been excluded from the merger, moved to Markinch and operated under the name of John Haig and Co. Ltd. The Cameron Bridge Distillery was the first to make bakers yeast by the improved Vienna Process which was an immediate success and won an award in 1886. During the 1960's DCL embarked on a programme of upgrading facilities and built a new boilerhouse, spirit store, still house and maltings. In 1986 the distillery was bought by Guinness and in 1989 another major investment involved moving a neutral spirit still from John Watney in London to Cameron Bridge. A third coffey still was also incorporated into the recently refurbished whisky still house. Beyond Cameron Bridge United Distillers, now the worlds largest spirits company, has a vast blending, bottling and warehouse complex. Finally Cameron Bridge House, built in 1849 for John Haig, was converted in 1911 into a hospital for infectious diseases.

HISTORIC TAYSIDE

Scotland is a country rich in the physical remains of her colourful past, many of which are in the care of Historic Scotland. This leaflet highlights a selection of sites in Tayside which are open for you to visit and enjoy.

CLAYPOTTS CASTLE

HISTORIC SCOTLAND

Thousands of years of history. Minutes from your door.

CLAYPOTTS CASTLE (FRONT COVER)

Once the residence of John Graham of Claverhouse, "Bonnie Dundee," Claypotts was originally built in the late 16th century for the Strachan family. It is a most unusual and complete tower house with circular towers on diagonally opposite corners. Between Dundee and Broughty Ferry, off the A92.

ELCHO CASTLE

A handsome fortified mansion of 16th century date with a profusion of round and square towers. Built for the Wemyss family, it was designed with comfort as well as defence in mind. The original iron grilles protecting the windows are still in place. On the River Tay 3 miles SE of Perth off the A912.

ARBROATH ABBEY

Arbroath Abbey holds a very special place in Scottish history for it was here in 1320 that the assembled Scottish nobles swore their independence from England in the famous "Declaration of Arbroath". Founded by King William the Lion of Scotland in 1178 whose tomb is within the abbey. In Arbroath town centre.

EDZELL CASTLE AND GARDEN

The beautiful walled garden at Edzell is one of Scotland's unique sights, created by Sir David Lindsay in 1604. The "Pleasance" is a delightful formal garden whose walls are decorated with sculptured stone panels and punctuated with recesses for flower boxes and nesting birds. Edzell Castle is the ancient seat of the Crawford Lindsays. At Edzell 6 miles N of Brechin on the B966.

HUNTINGTOWER CASTLE

The castle is made up of two fine and complete towers, built in the 15th and 16th centuries and then joined together in the 17th century. It belonged to the Ruthven family who were at the forefront of Scottish history in the 16th century. The castle contains a number of fine painted ceilings and is 3 miles NW of Perth off the A85.

MEIGLE SCULPTURED STONES

A remarkable collection of 25 sculptured monuments of the Celtic Christian period, housed in the old school in Meigle. This is one of the finest collections of Dark Age sculpture in Western Europe. In Meigle on the A94.

Opening times: April-September, Mon-Sat 9.30am-7pm, Sun 2pm-7pm; October-March, Mon-Sat 9.30am-4pm; Sun 2pm-4pm. Claypotts and Elcho close in winter, other properties may close for a day and a half. Telephone 031-244 3101 to check winter opening for a specific property.

For further information on all of the properties under our protection or for an application form to become one of our many Friends, please contact us at the address below:

Historic Scotland, 20 Brandon Street, Edinburgh EH3 5RA. Tel: 031-244 3101 (Monday-Friday 9am-5pm)

SKEW PUTT, BAY HOUSE, DYSART.

PLACES

PCAD♡1728
(MARRIAGE LINTEL, KINGHORN)

BIBLIOGRAPHY

A History of Glenrothes - Keith Ferguson
Auld Buckhyne - Frank Rankin
Bygone Fife - James Wilkie
Bygone Leven & Bygone Kirkcaldy - Eric Eunson
Chapel Shore Trail - West Wemyss
Coaltown of Wemyss - Wemyss Env. Education Centre
Discovering Fife - Raymond Lamont Brown
Dysart - Past and Present - A.S. Cunningham
Glenrothes & its environment - WG Rowntree
Kennoway & the fringes of Markinch - A.S. Cunningham
Kennoway - Den & Town - Kennoway Primary School
Kinghorn - Alan Reid.
Kirkcaldy Burgh Boundary - Kirkcaldy Civic Society
Kirkcaldy in a Nutshell - Kirkcaldy Civic Society
Kirkcaldy Walkabouts - Pathhead - Kirkcaldy Civic Soc.
Leven and Silverburn Walkabout - Levenmouth Env. Soc.
Macduff Castle - Frank Rankin
Methil - History and Trail - Mary Cameron
Milton of Balgonie - Village History and Walks Around
The Buildings of Scotland - Fife - John Gifford.
The Dysart Trail - The Dysart Trust
The Kingdom of Fife - Theo Lang
The Lang Toun - Jack House
The Lion in the North - John Prebble
The Wemyss Caves - Frank Rankin
Thornton Village History and Walks Around - W.E.E.C.
Windygates, Balcurvie and Cameron Bridge - A. Dickson

THE BULL STONE, LESLIE

ACKNOWLEDGEMENTS

I am grateful to many local people for their help in providing old books and photographs during the research for this book. In particular many thanks to staff at the Kirkcaldy District Council Tourist Information Offices and Public Libraries; Mr & Mrs McIntosh, Windygates; Mrs Robertson for permission to sketch the doocot at Bow Butts House, Kinghorn; and to my parents - Tom & Betty Pearson. I am also grateful for assistance given by Mr & Mrs T. Herd of The New Caledonian Hotel, Leven.

J.M.P.

47

KIRKCALDY DISTRICT COUNCIL
COAT OF ARMS

The Author

John MacMillan Pearson was born at St. Andrews, Fife in 1952. He is an architect by profession having graduated with a Bachelor of Architecture degree at Heriot-Watt University, Edinburgh in 1976. Travelled overseas between 1977-1983 to Japan and the Far East and worked in Australia and New Zealand before returning to Scotland. Developed a keen interest in sketching and calligraphy through meeting the Canadian artist Barbara Elizabeth Mercer. From 1983-1987 he worked for the Edinburgh architects' firm Dick Peddie and McKay at their Invergordon office. Has since completed a five year stint in the London area while working on an office development at Harrow.

Other publications by J.M. Pearson:

A Guided Walk round Inverness
A Guided Walk round St. Andrews
A Guided Walk round Edinburgh
Around North East Fife
Burntisland
St. Andrews - Street Map & Places of Interest
Edinburgh - The Royal Mile Guide

Above publications available from:-
J.M.Pearson, 'Lingmoor,' Carberry Park, Leven, Fife. KY8 4JG. Books £3.50 (inc.P&P).

INDUSTRY

1887

Durie Street, Leven.

48